H ____ G

FOR THE NATIONS

BY

DR. GERTRUDE DIXON

Fairmont Books is a ministry of The McDougal Foundation, Inc., a Maryland nonprofit corporation dedicated to spreading the Gospel of the Lord Jesus Christ to as many people as possible in the shortest time possible.

Published by:

Fairmont Books
P.O. Box 3595
Hagerstown, MD 21742-3595

ISBN 1-884369-92-8

Printed in the United States of America
For Worldwide Distribution

DEDICATION

In memory of my father, Watson Brown, Sr., and my mother Annie Mae Brown, who taught me so much and gave me such a solid foundation for my life. I thank God for the godly heritage they gave me. They are gone home to be with the Lord, but if they were here to see this book, they would see it as part of the harvest from their years of sowing.

To my husband, Joseph B. T. Dixon, Jr., for his love and support in standing with me in whatever God tells me to do.

To our daughter Joyce Bowie, and our grandsons, Steve Bowie and Shihee H. Bowie.

To my sisters and brothers, Dr. Rose M. Brown, Alonzo Brown, Samuel Brown and Linda Brown.

ACKNOWLEDGMENTS

Special thanks to my Lord and Savior, Jesus Christ, who spoke to me with His power from on high to write this book.

Thanks to my husband, Joseph B. T. Dixon, Jr., for his love and support in standing with me in whatever God tells me to do.

Thanks to my sister, Dr. Rose Marie Brown, for her love, prayers, support and willingness to listen.

Special thanks to Sister Shirley Maynard and to my church members for their love, support and prayers.

Special thanks to Rev. Harold McDougal for his professional editing of this manuscript and to his beautiful wife, Sister Diane McDougal, for all she does to make these book projects a reality.

Special thanks to all my friends and prayer partners who have prayed for me and my family through the years.

Special thanks to Reverend Ruth Naomi Matteiss and the Williamsport Church for their love and prayers.

Special thanks to Mrs. Beulah Wilk for all of her love, support and prayers.

CONTENTS

And he showed me a pure river of water of life, clear as crystal, proceeding out of the throne of God and of the Lamb. In the midst of the street of it, and on either side of the river, was there the tree of life, which bare twelve manner of fruits, and yielded her fruit every month: and the leaves of the tree were FOR THE HEALING OF THE NATIONS. Revelation 22:1-2

INTRODUCTION

On the evening of our Independence Day celebration in July of 1996, just after I had left an anointed church service, the Lord spoke to me and said, "Write a book on *Healing for the Nations.*" I had been fasting all that day, and the power and anointing of God were so heavy upon me that it seemed it must be very much like what John experienced on the Isle of Patmos when he received his great revelation. I felt intoxicated, like the disciples on the Day of Pentecost. It was such an overwhelming experience that it is difficult to explain.

As the Lord spoke to me, He showed me that these are among the days of which the prophet Joel spoke when he said:

> *And it shall come to pass afterward, that I will pour out my spirit upon all flesh; and your sons and your daughters shall prophesy, your old men shall dream dreams, your young men shall see visions: And also upon the servants and upon the handmaids in those days will I pour out my spirit. ... And it shall come to pass, that whosoever shall call on the name of the LORD shall be delivered:*

for in mount Zion and in Jerusalem shall be de-
liverance, as the LORD hath said, and in the
remnant whom the LORD shall call.

Joel 2:28-29 and 32

When I looked at the world around me, most of what I saw was bad. Things didn't seem to be getting better, but worse. Violence and hatred, wars and strife seemed to be everywhere; yet God said He would pour out His Spirit in these last days and that wonderful things would happen on the Earth. He spoke of men and women, young and old alike, being filled with His Spirit and manifesting His power. How could this be possible?

I wrote down much of what God was showing me, but then I put it aside until a later date. I knew that surely there must be much more that I needed to understand of this revelation. How could God bring healing to the nations when those nations were in such turmoil and rebellion against Him?

That Saturday morning, the Lord woke me very early and began to speak to me again. "Many of My people are hurting, brokenhearted, crippled and ashamed," He told me. "They need someone to stand in the gap for them, to pray and intercede for the healing of the nations." I didn't go back to sleep that morning. Instead, I got up and sought God.

In the days that followed days I spent time in intense prayer, seeking the Lord for His will. As I did so, I began to see the world through His eyes. He saw our planet, our nations, as sick and corrupted, damaged and torn, oppressed and in captivity. Yet I saw His hands extended toward the whole world, toward this nation and all the nations, and I saw the look of love in His eyes as He reached out to anyone willing to receive Him.

I sensed Him saying, "My people shall be set free, healed and delivered from their oppression and hurts. Their blind eyes shall be opened. The lame shall walk, the dumb shall speak, and those who are in captivity shall come forth." It was almost more than I could comprehend. After I had written down all that I could remember of what the Lord was saying, I laid my pages aside, but God's message to me during that time was never forgotten.

In November of 1997 God began to speak to me once more concerning this theme. Again I was overwhelmed by the power of the Spirit I felt, and again I sensed that I must somehow put God's thoughts into a book. Although the world was in terrible shape, I was made to know that if God's people would pray and seek His face, wonderful things would happen.

After writing down all the Lord had spoken to me concerning this theme, I submitted the manuscript to my publisher. I was sure, when the book was published, that God would help me get it into the hands of those who need to read it. And He has faithfully done just that.

God is ready to extend *Healing for the Nations*. Receive it. I trust that this message will bring healing to you, to your family, to your community and to your nation.

Dr. Gertrude Dixon
Hagerstown, Maryland

PART I:

THE SICKNESS

ONE

THE NATIONS ARE SICK AND DESPERATELY NEED TO BE HEALED

Come, and let us return unto the LORD.

Hosea 6:1

*I*t is time for the Church here in America and around the world to rise up. It is time for her to proclaim that the Lord is God, and that if we will obey Him, He has answers for our troubled time. It is time to rise up in purity and righteousness, to cease from wallowing in the mire of the sin that surrounds us. Nations are in peril. Sin is rampant and godliness seems sometimes difficult to find. Isaiah might have been speaking to the United States or another of our modern nations rather than to Israel when he said:

Ah sinful nation, a people laden with iniquity, a seed of evildoers, children that are corrupters: they have forsaken the LORD, they have provoked the Holy One of Israel unto anger, they are gone away backward. Why should ye be stricken any more? ye will revolt more and more: the whole head is sick, and the whole heart faint. From the sole of the foot even unto the head there is no soundness in it; but wounds, and bruises, and putrifying sores: they have not been closed, neither bound up, neither mollified with ointment.

Isaiah 1:4-6

Child abuse, divorce, juvenile crime, drug and alcohol addiction, murder, abortion, teenage pregnancy, arson, theft, suicide, war, homelessness and abject poverty ... these are but a few of the symptoms of our sick society. Even the wisest political and social leaders of our day often throw up their hands in dismay because of the difficulty of dealing with the problems that we now confront on a daily basis. As a Christian counselor, I have heard almost everything there is to hear, and I can tell you that this is a dark hour for the nation and the world.

No matter where we happen to live on this Earth, there are plenty of problems all around us, many of them serious. No one is contesting that fact. The nations and their people are sick and need to be healed. They are possessed of satanic spirits and need to be set free. That these satanic spirits are real there is no doubt, for the fruits of their vile labors are manifested all around us. Those who deny these problems must be wandering about with blinders. Evil forces have bound far too many people and have caused them to do detestable things. Satan is using the most horrible means to destroy our children one by one before our very eyes.

So many people are sick today that we would have to call it a plague, a crisis of spiritual health. Whole families are sick, whole communities are sick, and whole nations are sick. The nations of this world are sick and desperately need to be healed. Corruption and immorality seem to be sweeping the entire planet, bringing with them this veritable plague of human suffering.

The sickness of our age has even affected some servants of the Lord. Many pastors, evangelists, missionaries and others in important leadership positions in the Church have stopped preaching the Gospel. Many of them have fallen into sin themselves and have compromised their message for the sake of money, fame, houses, cars or illicit relationships.

Jesus foretold this troubled period. He said it would be a time of father against son and son against father; mother against daughter and daughter against mother; mother-in-law against daughter-in-law and daughter-in-law against mother-in-law. He warned us that this would be a sign of the times we were living in and that we should be careful not to be overcome by it, but prepare to meet the Lord, for the end is near.

The chaos which envelops modern society is not what God envisioned or purposed when He created man. Somehow God's glorious creation has gone terribly wrong. He created us to live in joy and abundance. He intended that we have health, happiness and prosperity. He proclaimed that we should *"eat the good of the land"* (Isaiah 1:19). What has happened? And what, if anything, can we do about it?

Let us ask God today to help us become instruments of *Healing for the Nations.*

THE NATIONS CAN BE HEALED BECAUSE WE CAN IDENTIFY THE SICKNESS

Righteousness exalteth a nation: but sin is a reproach to any people.   Proverbs 14:34

*W*hat makes a child shoot his classmates? What brings a young woman to subject her unborn child to crack addiction? What causes teenagers to run away from home and get involved with the wrong crowd? Even the professionals of our modern era sometimes find it difficult to explain the rash actions of some.

Why are our families breaking apart in such large numbers? Why is there such a high incidence of divorce in the "enlightened" nations of the world? Why do new sicknesses crop up all around us? There are many other difficult questions that we could ask.

The scene before us is not a pleasant one, but the wonderful thing is that there is hope. These problems can be resolved if we will only recognize what causes them and be willing to treat it. The Bible has answers to all of these questions, and the simple answer is that the cause of the sickness we are witnessing all around us is sin. As old-fashioned as that concept may seem, there is no other answer. As much as we might like to find a more modern name for the problem, it is not to be found.

The wise King Solomon wrote these words: "*Righteousness exalteth a nation: but sin is a reproach to any people*" (Proverbs 14:30 and 34). This truth is confirmed in many other scriptural teachings. Solomon called the sin of envy, for instance, "*the rottenness of the bones.*"

What is sin? It is disobedience of God. It is lawlessness, unrighteousness. It is doing what we should not be doing or failing to do what we should be doing. Sin is the cause of moral sickness and can cause physical sickness as well. Sin always leads to sickness and, if sin is left unchecked, it even leads to death:

> *For the wages of sin is death; but the gift of God is eternal life through Jesus Christ our Lord.*
> Romans 6:23

The Nations Can Be Healed

For as often as ye eat this bread, and drink this cup, ye do show the Lord's death till he come. Wherefore whosoever shall eat this bread, and drink this cup of the Lord, unworthily, shall be guilty of the body and blood of the Lord. But let a man examine himself, and so let him eat of that bread, and drink of that cup. For he that eateth and drinketh unworthily, eateth and drinketh damnation to himself, not discerning the Lord's body. For this cause many are weak and sickly among you, and many sleep.

1 Corinthians 11:26-30

This principle is just as true for individuals as it is for families, communities and nations. Sin has separated us from God, and sin has brought upon us its myriad evils.

"Could sin be the cause of homelessness?" some might ask. Absolutely!

"Could sin be the cause of financial difficulties?" Yes, it could!

"Could sin be the cause of wars?" Most definitely!

Does this mean that we should not help those who find themselves in difficulties since, after all, sin is at the root of their problem? No! That is all the more reason to reach out to them.

I am not saying that every problem is linked to some particular sin a person has committed. We cannot say, for example, "You sinned, and therefore you lost your home. Too bad!" Sin has a cumulative affect. We have all sinned. We all make wrong choices. We have all chosen to disobey God at one time or another. We have no right, therefore, to look down on anyone else. Christ has been merciful to us, and He has called us to extend mercy to others. Jesus tried to instill this attitude in His disciples:

> *There were present at that season some that told him of the Galilaeans, whose blood Pilate had mingled with their sacrifices. And Jesus answering said unto them, Suppose ye that these Galilaeans were sinners above all the Galilaeans, because they suffered such things? I tell you, Nay: but, except ye repent, ye shall all likewise perish. Or those eighteen, upon whom the tower in Siloam fell, and slew them, think ye that they were sinners above all men that dwelt in Jerusalem? I tell you, Nay: but, except ye repent, ye shall all likewise perish.*
> Luke 13:1-5

In another instance, the Lord healed a man born blind whom the disciples did not regard as worthy of His touch:

> *And as Jesus passed by, he saw a man which was blind from his birth. And his disciples asked him, saying, Master, who did sin, this man, or his parents, that he was born blind? Jesus answered,*

The Nations Can Be Healed

Neither hath this man sinned, nor his parents: but that the works of God should be made manifest in him.   John 9:1-3

Make no mistake, sin brings punishment, and some people are sick or in difficulty because of the sins they have committed. The sin that affects many, however, is not their own, but another's. A mother who has lost a child to a drunken driver may have done nothing to deserve such a fate, and her child may have been innocent. Still, the sin of the drunken driver touches both their lives, changing that family forever.

When a person lives righteously, everyone around him is blessed:

When it goeth well with the righteous, the city rejoiceth: and when the wicked perish, there is shouting. By the blessing of the upright the city is exalted.   Proverbs 11:10-11

This works the other way around as well. Sin adversely affects us all.

While it is true that we have all sinned (*"all have sinned, and come short of the glory of God,"* Romans 3:23) and that none of us is perfect, some have chosen sin as a way of life. Some have chosen to ignore God and to live in the way that pleases themselves. This was the mistake of Adam and Eve in the Garden. It was this sin that caused them to lose their exalted position in the Garden. It never pays to rebel against God.

Some sins are more serious than others. Some people actually replace the true and living God, the Creator of the Universe, with some other god — whether they name that god, or not. These people become idolaters by giving the best of their time and talents to a false god, and anything that replaces God in our devotion is a false god.

Sin of any kind, however, brings hideous effects. It destroys our relationship with God and with those around us. It destroys our health. It destroys our minds. If left unchecked, sin will eventually drag us down to Hell. If sin is not overcome it will eventually cause us to suffer the ultimate loss — the loss of our soul.

It is common knowledge that the first step in treating any illness is to recognize it, to diagnose it. Once a sickness has been successfully diagnosed, a proper course of treatment can then be prescribed. Because we know that the cause of society's present ills is sin, we have taken the first step toward *Healing for the Nations*. We know the problem. Now let us find the remedy.

THE NATIONS CAN BE HEALED BECAUSE WE KNOW THE REMEDY

Is there no balm in Gilead; is there no physician there? why then is not the health of the daughter of my people recovered? Jeremiah 8:22

*I*f we constantly focus on all the problems around us, we will never find a solution. In fact, if we concentrate on the problems, we will become discouraged and give up even trying to overcome the evils of the world. If we see only the problems, they will drag us down too. We must stop looking at the difficulties and start looking to the Solution. As Christians, we not only know the cause of the sickness, but we also know the Remedy. His

Name is Jesus. We can boldly answer the question of Jeremiah: Yes, there is a balm in Gilead. Yes, we have a Savior!

We serve an awesome God and nothing is impossible for Him. The condition of the nations is not the important thing and not the thing we must be focusing on. The important thing is that our God has not changed. His power is the same today as it ever was. Evil has always existed, but God's love has always outshined that evil. It is no different in the dawning of the twenty-first century. There is hope.

There is power in the name of Jesus, power in His blood, power in His Word. The song writer, A.H. Ackley, was inspired to write:

> *I serve a risen Savior,*
> *He's in the world today;*
> *I know that He is living,*
> *Whatever men may say;*
> *I see His hand of mercy,*
> *I hear His voice of cheer,*
> *And just the time I need Him*
> *He's always near.*

> CHORUS:
> *He lives, He lives,*
> *Christ Jesus lives today!*
> *He walks with me and talks with me*
> *Along life's narrow way.*

We Know the Remedy

He lives, He lives,
Salvation to impart!
You ask me how I know He lives?
He lives within my heart.   — A.H. Ackley

I believe I know just what Brother Ackley was feeling when he wrote that wonderful hymn. I feel the awesomeness of my God about me every day of my life. He is alive, He is in the world today, and it is a joy to serve Him. Even though we are living in this dark world, God's Spirit places joy within our hearts. Like the song writer, "I see His hand of mercy" and "I hear His voice of cheer," and "just the time I need Him, He's always near." Praise God, "He lives!"

Another song writer declared: "Just when I need Him, Jesus is near," while another was inspired to write, "And He walks with me, and He talks with me, and He tells me I am His own."

It is astounding to know that in the midst of this sin-cursed world, we can experience the greatness of the blessing of God. He not only saves us from the curse of the world, but we become His children and walk and talk with Him. He shares with us things that we could not even think of with our limited understanding. Oh, what a mighty God we serve! There is none like Him in all the Earth! His love *"passes knowledge"* (Ephesians 3:19).

The remedy to the ills of this world is ever the

same: the answer is found in Christ Jesus. As another song writer said, "My Father is rich in houses and lands." All of creation still belongs to Him, regardless of Satan's lies:

The earth is the LORD'S, and the fulness thereof; the world, and they that dwell therein.

Psalm 24:1

All that we could possibly need, God already has, and He knows that we need it:

Be not ye therefore like unto them: for your Father knoweth what things ye have need of, before ye ask him. Matthew 6:8

Jesus promised us:

And all things, whatsoever ye shall ask in prayer, believing, ye shall receive. Matthew 21:22

Since our God has everything we need, all we have to do is ask Him in faith. He is waiting for our call. When we can wake up to these facts, Christ will give us light:

Wherefore he saith, Awake thou that sleepest, and arise from the dead, and Christ shall give thee light. Ephesians 5:14

We Know the Remedy

What is the remedy for sin? It is to be found in Christ Jesus. When we confess our sin and repent of it, turning from sin and embracing Jesus and His way for our lives, He washes us in the blood He shed for us at the cross. Then we are free to walk without sin. This is true for Christians as well as non-Christians:

> *But if we walk in the light, as he is in the light, we have fellowship one with another, and the blood of Jesus Christ his Son cleanseth us from all sin. If we say that we have no sin, we deceive ourselves, and the truth is not in us. If we confess our sins, he is faithful and just to forgive us our sins, and to cleanse us from all unrighteousness.*
> 1 John 1:7-9

We know the remedy for the problems our world is facing. It is Christ Jesus and we embrace His love. Let us now walk in this light, spreading its splendor to those around us. In this way, we can bring forth *Healing for the Nations*.

PART II:

THE MEANS FOR HEALING

THE POWER OF
INTERCESSORY PRAYER

*And I sought for a man among them, that should
make up the hedge, and stand in the gap before
me for the land, that I should not destroy it: but I
found none.*   Ezekiel 22:30

As believers, one of our most im-
portant privileges is that of prayer. We are called to
be a people of prayer, and a large part of our prayer
life should be spent in intercessory prayer. By inter-
ceding for one another and for the nation, we
literally *"bear one another's burdens"* in prayer, lift-
ing the needs of others before the Lord and gaining,
for them, the desired victory.

31

Prayer then is probably the most important thing we can do to bring healing to our nation and the world. Prayer is our most important weapon against the enemy and his ways. Someone must be found who will *"stand in the gap."*

We know that God will hear us when we come before Him. The Apostle Paul taught:

Be careful for nothing; but in every thing by prayer and supplication with thanksgiving let your requests be made known unto God. And the peace of God, which passeth all understanding, shall keep your hearts and minds through Christ Jesus. Philippians 4:6-7

Our part is to come to God, making known our requests, and His part is to do the work. If we do our part, He is always faithful to do His.

Do you desire that a loved one come to know Christ? Then pray.

Do you want to see revival in your local church? Then pray.

Do you want to be a part of what God is doing all over the nation and the world? Then pray.

Pray for repentance, for new life, for revival. Pray for the healing of this nation and pray for the healing of the nations.

Prayer can be hard work, so many don't want to participate. Those who choose to be used in intercessory prayer must be faithful to it, praying without ceasing and without doubting, praying in the knowledge that God hears and answers and that every effort put forth in prayer is worthwhile.

What is happening when it sometimes seems that God is not hearing and answering our prayers, either for ourselves or for others? We must simply trust Him and turn the results over to Him. He knows our hearts, and He understands our doubts and fears. He also understands every situation much better than we do. If we will persevere, not allowing the devil to convince us that God is not about to answer us, that He doesn't care for us and that prayer doesn't accomplish anything, then we will be blessed as we watch God at work for us.

Our prayers will certainly become targets for the devil, and he will try to interfere with their fulfillment. It has always been so, for he wants to hinder God's work. It was so for our first parents in the Garden, it was so for the prophet Daniel, and it will be so for us.

The devil will try every way he can to make your prayers powerless. He will attempt to cause you to doubt and fear or to become impatient. But do not worry about Satan, and do not listen to his lies. Maintain a proper attitude of faith, confessing any lack of faith and asking for strength, and God will answer your prayers — no matter what Satan does.

One important aspect of intercession is fasting.

We can fast before the Lord as a means of focusing our prayers while denying the flesh. Isaiah wrote perhaps the most well known passage concerning fasting in the Scriptures:

> *Cry aloud, spare not, lift up thy voice like a trumpet, and show my people their transgression, and the house of Jacob their sins. Yet they seek me daily, and delight to know my ways, as a nation that did righteousness, and forsook not the ordinance of their God: they ask of me the ordinances of justice; they take delight in approaching to God. Wherefore have we fasted, say they, and thou seest not? wherefore have we afflicted our soul, and thou takest no knowledge? Behold, in the day of your fast ye find pleasure, and exact all your labours. Behold, ye fast for strife and debate, and to smite with the fist of wickedness: ye shall not fast as ye do this day, to make your voice to be heard on high. Is it such a fast that I have chosen? a day for a man to afflict his soul? is it to bow down his head as a bulrush, and to spread sackcloth and ashes under him? wilt thou call this a fast, and an acceptable day to the* LORD? Isaiah 58:1-5

This passage describes a person who is fasting but is not doing it in a righteous way or for a righteous purpose. This person does not have a real attitude of prayer, but rather of self-righteousness. The prophet goes on to contrast man's shallow ideas of fasting with the true fast that God requires:

> *Is not this the fast that I have chosen? to loose the bands of wickedness, to undo the heavy burdens, and to let the oppressed go free, and that ye break every yoke? Is it not to deal thy bread to the hungry, and that thou bring the poor that are cast out to thy house? when thou seest the naked, that thou cover him; and that thou hide not thyself from thine own flesh? Then shall thy light break forth as the morning, and thine health shall spring forth speedily: and thy righteousness shall go before thee; the glory of the LORD shall be thy rereward. Then shalt thou call, and the LORD shall answer; thou shalt cry, and he shall say, Here I am. If thou take away from the midst of thee the yoke, the putting forth of the finger, and speaking vanity; And if thou draw out thy soul to the hungry, and satisfy the afflicted soul; then shall thy light rise in obscurity, and thy darkness be as the noon day: And the LORD shall guide thee continually, and satisfy thy soul in drought, and make fat thy bones: and thou shalt be like a watered garden, and like a spring of water, whose waters fail not.*
>
> Isaiah 58:6-11

Our fast is to be a righteous fast. It is not enough just to abstain from food. We must also embrace the practice of righteousness. Our fasting must not be hypocritical. Through the prophet Isaiah, God reproved such hypocrisy. Let your fasting please the heart of God.

As you fast, pray for revival. Pray for people to be delivered and set free. Pray for believers everywhere that they will shine forth as bright lights in the world. Paul urged the Ephesian believers to pray for him in this way:

> *Praying always with all prayer and supplication in the Spirit, and watching thereunto with all perseverance and supplication for all saints; And for me, that utterance may be given unto me, that I may open my mouth boldly, to make known the mystery of the gospel, For which I am an ambassador in bonds: that therein I may speak boldly, as I ought to speak.* Ephesians 6:18-20

Draw close to God and seek His face diligently as you intercede, and your reward will be great.

The prophet Nehemiah was a man of prayer who interceded for his people. When word reached him of some serious problems back home, he was deeply moved by it and sought God:

> *And it came to pass in the month Chisleu, in the twentieth year, as I was in Shushan the palace, That Hanani, one of my brethren, came, he and*

certain men of Judah; and I asked them concerning the Jews that had escaped, which were left of the captivity, and concerning Jerusalem. And they said unto me, The remnant that are left of the captivity there in the province are in great affliction and reproach: the wall of Jerusalem also is broken down, and the gates thereof are burned with fire. And it came to pass, when I heard these words, that I sat down and wept, and mourned certain days, and fasted, and prayed before the God of heaven. Nehemiah 1:1-4

Nehemiah *"wept and mourned ... and fasted and prayed,"* and God is calling for some more Nehemiahs to intercede for our generation.

Nehemiah did something else. Even though he apparently walked in righteousness himself, he fell on his face before God in repentance for the sins of the nation as a whole:

I beseech thee, O LORD God of heaven, the great and terrible God, that keepeth covenant and mercy for them that love him and observe his commandments: Let thine ear now be attentive, and thine eyes open, that thou mayest hear the prayer of thy servant, which I pray before thee now, day and night, for the children of Israel thy servants, and confess the sins of the children of Israel, which we have sinned against thee: both I and my father's house have sinned. Nehemiah 1:5-6

Healing for the Nations

Nehemiah's prayer was like healing oil poured into the wounds that sin had inflicted upon the nation of Israel. This prayer of repentance for the sins of the people was the beginning of a new move of God in the nation. He had a burden and he carried that burden to God in prayer. Ultimately, he helped to lead the people, not only to spiritual restoration, but in restoring the walls of the Holy City as well.

What are the sins of your nation? Think of them: murder, abortion, drug abuse, lying, rampant materialism, sexual uncleanness or perversion, violence. You may have others to add to the list. Pray over these sins, allowing the Spirit of the Lord to show you how to intercede on behalf of the people. You may not have been involved personally with many or even any of these sins, but you can stand before God on behalf of your nation and your people.

What is the sin from which all others spring? It is a turning away from God, a rejection of God and all He is and stands for. Cry out to God for your nation and seek His forgiveness for this root of all ills. Believe God for multitudes from among your fellow nationals to turn to Christ in repentance.

We need many more Nehemiahs today, more intercessors who will care for the people and the nation and will pay a price in prayer for the welfare of everyone. This is the first step toward bring restoration to our land and healing to the nations.

The Power of Intercessory Prayer

Churches must unite in prayer. It is time that we come together in love and respect for one another, as the Bible directs. We are different people with different opinions, but we can still love one another and respect one another. Even if we cannot agree on every principle of doctrine, let us unite for the sake of the nation and for the sake of our children and grandchildren. Let us believe God to make our nation a better place to live. Only God can bring it about, but He will if we are faithful in our role as intercessors.

Jeremiah also cried out to God on behalf of his people:

Why then is this people of Jerusalem slidden back by a perpetual backsliding? they hold fast deceit, they refuse to return. I hearkened and heard, but they spake not aright: no man repented him of his wickedness, saying, What have I done? every one turned to his course, as the horse rusheth into the battle. Yea, the stork in the heaven knoweth her appointed times; and the turtle and the crane and the swallow observe the time of their coming; but my people know not the judgment of the LORD. ... When I would comfort myself against sorrow, my heart is faint in me. Behold the voice of the cry of the daughter of my people because of them that dwell in a far country: Is not the LORD in Zion? is not her king in her? Why have they provoked

me to anger with their graven images, and with
strange vanities? The harvest is past, the sum-
mer is ended, and we are not saved. For the hurt
of the daughter of my people am I hurt; I am black;
astonishment hath taken hold on me.
                              Jeremiah 8:5-7 and 18-21

The prophet was overcome with grief for his
people. He understood that as drought in the grow-
ing season makes hunger inevitable, so the passing
days without repentance in Judah made destruction
inevitable. He cried out for relief for his people. Their
wounds from sin seemed to be incurable, yet he was
believing God for relief:

> *For the hurt of the daughter of my people am I*
> *hurt; I am black; astonishment hath taken hold*
> *on me. Is there no balm in Gilead; is there no phy-*
> *sician there? why then is not the health of the*
> *daughter of my people recovered? Oh that my head*
> *were waters, and mine eyes a fountain of tears,*
> *that I might weep day and night for the slain of*
> *the daughter of my people!*   Jeremiah 8:21-9:1

Jeremiah so mourned the desperate state of the
Jewish people that he became known as "the weep-
ing prophet." Not only had the people sinned once,
but they seemed to be continually backsliding. This
was, for the prophet, dismaying. He could feel God's

love for the people, and His sadness that the people had turned from Him, their only Source of healing.

Our time is no different, and God is calling believers throughout America and the world to come together and pray for the healing balm of God to be poured out upon their respective nations. As Americans, let us believe God for our President, our Congress, our judges, and for every person in position of authority. Those of you who are in other countries, you can do the same for your people. The powerful God of Jeremiah's day is still alive. He is still doing great and mighty things for those who love Him. And He is calling us to be willing to make the sacrifice of time and energy necessary to come together and pray. He said:

> *If my people, which are called by my name, shall humble themselves, and pray, and seek my face, and turn from their wicked ways; then will I hear from heaven, and will forgive their sin, and will heal their land.*　　　　2 Chronicles 7:14

That promise is just as valid today as it ever was in days gone by. Through the ministry of intercessory prayer, we can bring forth *Healing for the Nations.*

FIVE

THE POWER OF
SPIRITUAL WARFARE

The Spirit of the Lord is upon me, because he hath anointed me to preach the gospel to the poor; he hath sent me to heal the brokenhearted, to preach deliverance to the captives, and recovering of sight to the blind, to set at liberty them that are bruised, To preach the acceptable year of the Lord.

Luke 4:18-19

*I*f we want to bring healing to our nation and the world, we must learn to go beyond mere intercession. God has called us to set people free. He has given us power to do battle with the enemy on behalf of individuals, communities, nations and entire continents. Satan has no right to enslave God's people, and our Lord's desire is to see others set free as well. The Bible says:

> *The earth is the LORD's, and the fulness thereof;*
> *the world, and they that dwell therein.*
>
> Psalm 24:1

It is time to take back what the enemy has robbed from us, to put him in his place and to declare liberty for the captives.

We have the right and the authority to speak light into people's lives and to pray deliverance over them. Even those who have not yet laid claim to Christ's promises for *"whosoever will"* are still His by right of creation. Though they do not yet know salvation, we can still believe and speak forth words of faith on their behalf.

Do we really have the authority to pray in this way? Yes, we do. This ministry is what people commonly call "doing spiritual warfare." The Scriptures are clear on this matter:

> *And I will give unto thee the keys of the kingdom*
> *of heaven: and whatsoever thou shalt bind on earth*
> *shall be bound in heaven: and whatsoever thou*
> *shalt loose on earth shall be loosed in heaven.*
>
> Matthew 16:19

> *Verily I say unto you, Whatsoever ye shall bind*
> *on earth shall be bound in heaven: and whatso-*

ever ye shall loose on earth shall be loosed in heaven. Again I say unto you, That if two of you shall agree on earth as touching any thing that they shall ask, it shall be done for them of my Father which is in heaven. For where two or three are gathered together in my name, there am I in the midst of them. Matthew 18:18-20

We have the authority in Christ to command evil spirits and forces of darkness to let God's people go in Jesus' Name. As we submit our hearts, lives and words to God, we can become a positive force to speak life into every situation.

This is called spiritual warfare because we actually do battle with demon spirits. Paul wrote to Timothy:

This charge I commit unto thee, son Timothy, according to the prophecies which went before on thee, that thou by them mightest war a good warfare. 1 Timothy 1:18

Satan has declared war on us, and if he can war against us, we can war against him too. It is time to sound the call to battle and declare war against the sin and the evil that is in the world. If we can stand firm against the enemy, we can take back the ground he has gained. We can be victors through the power of the blood of Christ, and we can bring forth and strengthen the Kingdom of Light on this Earth. Paul taught:

Put on the whole armour of God, that ye may be able to stand against the wiles of the devil. For we wrestle not against flesh and blood, but against principalities, against powers, against the rulers of the darkness of this world, against spiritual wickedness in high places. Wherefore take unto you the whole armour of God, that ye may be able to withstand in the evil day, and having done all, to stand. Stand therefore, having your loins girt about with truth, and having on the breastplate of righteousness; And your feet shod with the preparation of the gospel of peace; Above all, taking the shield of faith, wherewith ye shall be able to quench all the fiery darts of the wicked. And take the helmet of salvation, and the sword of the Spirit, which is the word of God.

Ephesians 6:11-17

God has destined us to win this war. Paul declared:

Nay, in all these things we are more than conquerors through him that loved us.

Romans 8:37

Get ready for battle. This will not be a battle against men, but against spiritual powers.

The Power of Spiritual Warfare

In his second letter to the Corinthians, Paul gave further instruction regarding spiritual warfare:

> *For though we walk in the flesh, we do not war after the flesh: (For the weapons of our warfare are not carnal, but mighty through God to the pulling down of strong holds;) Casting down imaginations, and every high thing that exalteth itself against the knowledge of God, and bringing into captivity every thought to the obedience of Christ.* 2 Corinthians 10:3-5

God is restoring to the Church gifts and ministries that were lost, and He has called us to participate in that restoration. We are to bring deliverance to the people so that God can fill them with His fullness.

Church, it is time to put the enemy in his place. We have the victory, for the devil is defeated! We are more than conquerors through Jesus Christ who loved us and gave Himself for us.

The work of deliverance is the work of bringing someone out of the kingdom of darkness and into the realm of Light. Christ Jesus ministered in this way, bringing peace and hope to those He helped and changing their lives forever.

God is raising up a ministry of deliverance today and is anointing those He has called to this ministry to break the yoke of sin in people's lives and to set the captives free. Those called to this ministry are anointed to set people free from demonic oppression and from the hold Satan has over their lives. God can use a chosen vessel mightily in this way, and this is a crucial ministry for our hour.

There is also a sense in which all believers can be ministers of deliverance. We can stand for others and help to set them free, regardless of our calling in life. As we live lives of righteousness in the world we touch the lives of those that need God. As we reveal Christ to others, He delivers them.

This is fitting, for Christ has delivered us:

> *[He] hath delivered us from the power of darkness, and hath translated us into the kingdom of his dear Son.*   Colossians 1:13

Because Christ has delivered us, we can now help bring deliverance to others. We are workers together with God for the salvation of lost souls around us. He is giving us a vision for their deliverance, and as we allow Christ to live His life through us, that life will touch others and enable them to be free. Let us go forth and proclaim *Healing for the Nations*.

THE POWER OF UNITY AMONG BELIEVERS

Neither pray I for these alone, but for them also which shall believe on me through their word; That they all may be one; as thou, Father, art in me, and I in thee, that they also may be one in us: that the world may believe that thou hast sent me. And the glory which thou gavest me I have given them; that they may be one, even as we are one: I in them, and thou in me, that they may be made perfect in one; and that the world may know that thou hast sent me, and hast loved them, as thou hast loved me. John 17:20-23

*J*ust before His death, Jesus was

praying in the garden, pouring out His heart to the Father one last time. He had prayed often during His time on Earth, but this prayer was somehow different. Jesus was not praying for great miracles and signs and wonders to be done among the believers. He was not praying for continual heavenly visions or prophetic words to come forth in their midst. He was not praying for material blessings to be loosed upon them. He was not even asking that His followers be spared physical or mental suffering. He was praying that His family would be united, that His people would become one Church.

The one thing on the heart of the Savior at that moment was not how church government would develop, whether or not members would be faithful in tithing or how they would perform the sacrament of water baptism. His burden was the coming together of His children, the unifying of His Body.

We are called to be one with Christ and one with our fellow Christians. Unity in the Body of Christ has always been God's intent. It was for the purpose of achieving unity that God placed a variety of ministries into the Body:

And he gave some, apostles; and some, prophets; and some, evangelists; and some, pastors and teachers; For the perfecting of the saints, for the work of the ministry, for the edifying of the body

The Power of Unity Among Believers

of Christ: Till we all come in the unity of the faith, and of the knowledge of the Son of God, unto a perfect man, unto the measure of the stature of the fulness of Christ. Ephesians 4:11-13

God is calling us to come into *"the unity of the faith."* Such a coming together would do more to bring God's blessing to this world that anything else we might do or say. The world is perplexed by the fact that "Christians" can't get along with each other while we all insist that we love Jesus.

Churches are splitting apart as much or more than they ever have in the past. Sometimes these divisions are caused by differences in doctrinal viewpoint, and sometimes they are caused by jealousies or personality clashes. Whatever the reasons for our divisions, can we not feel how it hurts the heart of God to see His children scattering and turning against each other? This should not be! While the Lord does not expect us all to be in agreement on every point, He does want to see us loving each other and helping each other.

Disagreement is not a sin. We can disagree and still get along. We can espouse differing traditions and still have fellowship with one another. Some might ask how this is possible? By focusing on the Lord Jesus instead of on our differences.

If a person believes in Jesus as the Son of God, if he has accepted God's offer of salvation, repenting and asking Jesus Christ to dwell in him, if he truly loves the Lord, then surely we can find some areas of agreement with that person. If he is saved, does it really matter exactly how he was baptized? Is that point important enough for me to break fellowship with him?

There are times when it is appropriate and necessary to discuss theology. There are times when it is necessary to study the Bible together, to see what the Word says about a given issue. But it is also all right to come away from these times with differing opinions. You can't always change your brother, so agree to disagree with him. It is not right to cut off fellowship with another believer because of insignificant doctrinal matters. This is not a time for creating more divisions. It is a time to come together. To prove this to us, God is sending a special anointing upon those who choose to unite.

The psalmist declared:

> *Behold, how good and how pleasant it is for brethren to dwell together in unity! It is like the precious ointment upon the head, that ran down upon the beard, even Aaron's beard: that went down to the skirts of his garments; As the dew of Hermon, and as the dew that descended upon the mountains of Zion: for there the LORD commanded the blessing, even life for evermore.*
>
> Psalm 133:1-3

The Power of Unity Among Believers

When we can learn to dwell together in unity, our joining becomes *"like the precious ointment"* of the Old Testament. It is a healing oil of God poured out upon us, upon those around us and upon the whole world.

If we Christians cannot come together without bringing with us our arguments, backbiting and envyings, what can we expect of the nation as a whole or of the world? The Church was predestined to be the light of the world. We are examples for others to follow. The life of Christ is in us and is shining forth from us for all the world to see. If we refuse to lay aside our petty differences and to love and help one another, what hope does the world have?

Each of us is certain that he or she is right about doctrinal matters so we insist on our own opinion. But we don't know everything, just as others don't know everything. Only God knows everything. Only God is perfect. Only God never errs. How can we allow our beliefs about a loving and compassionate God to cause contention and debate among us?

What will the coming judgment be like?
Who will go to Heaven?
What is the nature of Satan and of Hell?
Who will be part of the Bride of Christ and who will be her attendants?
What should Christians eat?
How should Christians dress?

These are all interesting points, but in the light of eternity, are they worth dividing the family and hurting the heart of God? The world is dying. Can we stop blaming each other long enough to care?

There is only *"one God,"* only *"one faith,"* and only *"one baptism,"* and we should all be able to build on that oneness. Paul wrote to the Ephesians:

> *I therefore, the prisoner of the Lord, beseech you that ye walk worthy of the vocation wherewith ye are called, With all lowliness and meekness, with longsuffering, forbearing one another in love; Endeavouring to keep the unity of the Spirit in the bond of peace. There is one body, and one Spirit, even as ye are called in one hope of your calling; One Lord, one faith, one baptism, One God and Father of all, who is above all, and through all, and in you all.* Ephesians 4:1-6

God is the *"Father of all,"* He is *"above all,"* He works *"through all,"* and He is *"in you all."* What does that word "all" mean? There is no other way to explain it. It means what it says: A L L.

God has not condemned men, and we must not condemn them either:

> *For God so loved the world, that he gave his only begotten Son, that whosoever believeth in him*

The Power of Unity Among Believers

should not perish, but have everlasting life. For
God sent not his Son into the world to condemn
the world; but that the world through him might
be saved. John 3:16-17

Jesus Christ, God's Son, was sent to be the sacrifice for the sins of the whole world because God loved us so much. That supreme sacrifice was made for all, and God accepts all who come to Him. He is not coming back for just one or two churches or denominations. He is coming back for all those whose robes have been washed in the blood of the Lamb.

How dare we try to alienate those whom God has called, simply because they dress differently or worship in a different style? God loves all His people and has a glorious end prepared for them. He has promised a great outpouring of His goodness just before He returns. Isaiah said:

For unto us a child is born, unto us a son is given:
and the government shall be upon his shoulder:
and his name shall be called Wonderful, Counsellor, The mighty God, The everlasting Father, The
Prince of Peace. Of the increase of his government
and peace there shall be no end, upon the throne
of David, and upon his kingdom, to order it, and
to establish it with judgment and with justice from
henceforth even for ever. The zeal of the LORD *of*
hosts will perform this. Isaiah 9:6-7

"Of the increase of His government and peace there shall be no end!" We know that we are part of that *"increase,"* and we must recognize that many other brothers are as well.

Walking in unity in no way implies that we should embrace every teaching or accept every prophecy that is brought forth. God has given us discernment and has called us to be men and women of His Word so that we can understand what the will of the Lord is.

Paul warned the Colossians:

Beware lest any man spoil you through philosophy and vain deceit, after the tradition of men, after the rudiments of the world, and not after Christ. For in him dwelleth all the fulness of the Godhead bodily. And ye are complete in him, which is the head of all principality and power: ... Let no man therefore judge you in meat, or in drink, or in respect of an holyday, or of the new moon, or of the sabbath days: Which are a shadow of things to come; but the body is of Christ. Let no man beguile you of your reward in a voluntary humility and worshipping of angels, intruding into those things which he hath not seen, vainly puffed up by his fleshly mind, And not holding the Head, from which all the body by joints and bands having nourishment ministered, and knit together, increaseth with the increase of God.

The Power of Unity Among Believers

Wherefore if ye be dead with Christ from the rudiments of the world, why, as though living in the world, are ye subject to ordinances, (Touch not; taste not; handle not; Which all are to perish with the using;) after the commandments and doctrines of men? Which things have indeed a show of wisdom in will worship, and humility, and neglecting of the body; not in any honour to the satisfying of the flesh.

Colossians 2:8-10 and 16-23

Just as there are true Christians who have power to bring healing to the nations, there are also false prophets and false teachers, and we must know the difference. If we are to bring God's blessing to our own nation and the world, we cannot be beguiled by the doctrines of men. They will rob us of our spiritual blessings. *"Stand fast,"* Paul admonished the Galatians:

Stand fast therefore in the liberty wherewith Christ hath made us free, and be not entangled again with the yoke of bondage. Galatians 5:1

We cannot allow ourselves to be carried away from the truth by false teaching, by a love of this world or by the religious teaching coming from the world's system. We must stand firm on what we know God's Word says.

Having said this, however, we must recognize that there are a vast number of fine Christian believers in the world today, and God is calling us to join hands with them to bring about *Healing for the Nations.*

THE POWER OF RIGHTEOUS LIVING

He that saith he abideth in him ought himself also
so to walk, even as he walked.   1 John 2:6

How can we expect to bless all nations if we can't first establish a pattern of righteous living in our own personal lives? If God is not working in us, then we have nothing to offer to others. If we are not first partakers of His goodness, why would others want what we have?

The problem we've had in recent years, when speaking of righteous living, is that Christians have begun to copy the unhealthy attitudes of the world around them. Instead of asking God to help them live righteously, they have started justifying their personal failures and blaming them on everyone else. Nowadays it seems that no one is responsible for anything. There is always someone else to blame, someone else to point the finger at.

Criminals are getting by with less and less punishment for horrible crimes these days because there is always a cause cited for their otherwise unjustifiable actions. If a person commits murder, they say it is because of something he suffered during his childhood. His act may also be blamed on a movie he watched, the lack of a father figure in the home, poverty or low status in society, or any number of other excuses. While all of these things can affect us, is it valid to assume that any of these may be the "cause" of a person killing another? What ever happened to personal responsibility and free will?

Until we stop justifying our actions and blaming everyone else but ourselves, we can never get better, never be rehabilitated, never change, never start living a righteous life. The removal of sin requires repentance, and repentance requires the acknowledgment of personal wrongdoing.

It is time for us to cry, "Enough!" We must start taking personal responsibility for the decisions we make in our lives.

God has given each of us a free will, and we can use that free will to live right or to live wrong. We can choose to follow after God, or we can choose to go the way of the world. If I choose to sin, then I have sinned, and it is not fair of me to blame someone else for that sin. It is true that many people who commit crimes grow up in poverty or in abusive situations, but it is also true that many others who grew up in similar situations have not committed any crimes at all. They have chosen another way.

As believers we must be the first to stand up and take responsibility for our actions, and when we do, the world will take notice. We are in charge of our daily decisions, and when we sin, it is because of our own wrong choices, not because of anyone or anything else. God is calling for a life of holiness, but it is our choice to make. We can live by His grace and power, making the choice not to sin. Sin is the easy way, but we must choose the higher way.

For some, time is quickly running out. We are living in the last days, and Christ is coming back soon. This is a time for us to walk holy before the Lord and to stop justifying sin. It is time for the Church to awaken from her slumber:

> *And that, knowing the time, that now it is high time to awake out of sleep: for now is our salvation nearer than when we believed. The night is far spent, the day is at hand: let us therefore cast off the works of darkness, and let us put on the armour of light. Let us walk honestly, as in the day; not in rioting and drunkenness, not in chambering and wantonness, not in strife and envying. But put ye on the Lord Jesus Christ, and*

> *make not provision for the flesh, to fulfil the lusts*
> *thereof.*   Romans 13:11-14

Church, we have a responsibility to fulfill — to God, to ourselves, to our churches and to the world. We were put here to be light and salt, to be examples and lead many to hope in Christ Jesus:

> *Ye are the salt of the earth: but if the salt have lost*
> *his savour, wherewith shall it be salted? it is*
> *thenceforth good for nothing, but to be cast out,*
> *and to be trodden under foot of men. Ye are the*
> *light of the world. A city that is set on an hill can-*
> *not be hid. Neither do men light a candle, and put*
> *it under a bushel, but on a candlestick; and it*
> *giveth light unto all that are in the house. Let your*
> *light so shine before men, that they may see your*
> *good works, and glorify your Father which is in*
> *heaven.*   Matthew 5:13-16

Let us lay aside every excuse and start living a righteous life. If we desire to bring healing to the nation, we must begin by being faithful to God in our personal lives.

Some would insist that it is impossible to live righteously, but they are mistaken. *"We can do all things through Christ."* We must learn to seek the Lord, to spend time in His Word and in prayer. He will help us, giving us the power to walk in love toward all, and to accomplish the ministry that He has placed in our hands. Through Him, we can shine forth the light of the glorious Gospel. Lay aside every excuse and begin to walk in righteousness before God.

These are *"evil"* days, but we can *"walk circumspectly"* in them:

> *See then that ye walk circumspectly, not as fools, but as wise, Redeeming the time, because the days are evil. Wherefore be ye not unwise, but understanding what the will of the Lord is. And be not drunk with wine, wherein is excess; but be filled with the Spirit; Speaking to yourselves in psalms and hymns and spiritual songs, singing and making melody in your heart to the Lord; Giving thanks always for all things unto God and the Father in the name of our Lord Jesus Christ; Submitting yourselves one to another in the fear of God.* Ephesians 5:15-21

We can overcome every temptation of the evil one by putting on *"the whole armor of God"*:

> *Put on the whole armour of God, that ye may be able to stand against the wiles of the devil. For we wrestle not against flesh and blood, but against principalities, against powers, against the rulers of the darkness of this world, against spiritual wickedness in high places. Wherefore take unto*

you the whole armour of God, that ye may be able to withstand in the evil day, and having done all, to stand. Stand therefore, having your loins girt about with truth, and having on the breastplate of righteousness; And your feet shod with the preparation of the gospel of peace; Above all, taking the shield of faith, wherewith ye shall be able to quench all the fiery darts of the wicked. And take the helmet of salvation, and the sword of the Spirit, which is the word of God: Praying always with all prayer and supplication in the Spirit, and watching thereunto with all perseverance and supplication for all saints.   Ephesians 6:11-18*

Righteous living must be exhibited not only in our individual lives, but in our families. The Scriptures have much to say about the manner in which we should conduct our most intimate relationships. It speaks to spouses, to parents and to children. We would do well to heed its admonitions. Paul, for instance, wrote:

Wives, submit yourselves unto your own husbands, as it is fit in the Lord.

Husbands, love your wives, and be not bitter against them.

Children, obey your parents in all things: for this is well pleasing unto the Lord.

The Power of Righteous Living

Fathers, provoke not your children to anger, lest they be discouraged.

And whatsoever ye do, do it heartily, as to the Lord, and not unto men; Knowing that of the Lord ye shall receive the reward of the inheritance: for ye serve the Lord Christ.

Colossians 3:18-21, 23-24

The proper relationship between husband and wife was emphasized in Paul's letter to the Church at Ephesus:

Wives, submit yourselves unto your own husbands, as unto the Lord. For the husband is the head of the wife, even as Christ is the head of the church: and he is the saviour of the body. Therefore as the church is subject unto Christ, so let the wives be to their own husbands in every thing. Husbands, love your wives, even as Christ also loved the church, and gave himself for it; That he might sanctify and cleanse it with the washing of water by the word, That he might present it to himself a glorious church, not having spot, or wrinkle, or any such thing; but that it should be holy and without blemish. So ought men to love their wives as their own bodies. He that loveth his wife loveth himself. Ephesians 5:22-28

Much has been taught and written concerning the need for wives to submit to their husbands. It should be pointed out that submission is not the same as servitude.

It sometimes seems that men have the more difficult of the two biblical directives. Theirs is not to follow, but to lead. How are they to do this? By loving their wives as Christ loves the Church. What a powerful example to follow! Men are to love their wives unconditionally. There is no loophole.

If men would truly follow their part of this passage, there would be no question as to whether or not submission is a difficult and degrading matter. A man who loves his wife in this way will not demean her, nor be cruel to her, nor be unfairly demanding of her. He will allow his love for her to lead him and he will earnestly seek God's best for his family.

If all the members of a family are seeking Him and following after Him, then family life will flow much more smoothly. There will still be problems, of course, but they will be fewer and will be resolved more easily.

I believe that God is calling men to arise and to take their rightful place in the home. They are to take back the spiritual leadership within the family that God has given to them. In a former time, families gathered around the table and the father of the household offered a blessing over the food. In a former time fathers prayed for and with their children each evening. In a former time, fathers set a godly example for their children to follow. Let's get back to those godly customs. Men should stop staying in the spiritual background and pushing their wives out front. Men, you are called by God to take the lead.

This does not mean that women cannot excel. Many women hold positions of authority in business and politics throughout this and many other nations, and God is raising up great women leaders in our churches. That's God's business. He raises up whom He will. This should not stop any man from doing what he was called to do. A real woman of God wants her husband to stand up and take his rightful place in the family. She wants to be able to look up to him and proudly say, "I want you to meet my husband." She doesn't want to have to lead him along like a puppy dog.

Often, when men complain that their wives will not submit to them, it is because they are not leading the family. Submit to what? There is nothing to submit to. It is time for change in this area, as God brings healing and restoration to our families.

This struggle to once again win our families is just that — a struggle. The enemy does not want Christians to have strong, healthy families because he doesn't want the power and the goodness of God to be shown forth clearly to the world.

If we are to maintain our families strong and spiritually sound, the truths we have cited concerning intercessory prayer and spiritual warfare must first be applied to our own loved ones. Always remember the words of Saint Paul: *"We wrestle not against flesh and blood"*! Our fight is not against our spouses, our parents, or our children. Our families are on our side! Rather, our fight is against the devil, against the invisible powers that would threaten our families. Don't ever allow Satan to convince you that people are the problem when trouble arises. Our battle is not against those we love, but against the enemy of our souls.

A great responsibility rests upon all believers to raise their children to be men and women of God. This is not a priority for many. In this age of abortion on demand, soaring levels of out-of-wedlock births and child abuse, we should recall what the Scriptures have to say about children:

> *Lo, children are an heritage of the LORD: and the fruit of the womb is his reward. As arrows are in the hand of a mighty man; so are children of the youth. Happy is the man that hath his quiver full of them: they shall not be ashamed, but they shall speak with the enemies in the gate.*
>
> Psalm 127:3-5

Children are a gift from God! They are not burdens to be borne the best we can. They are not inconveniences. They need not interfere with our lives. This is the attitude of our modern world. God says that they are His precious gifts to us.

Many are going through trials with their children, and sometimes it is our own fault. Our child cannot respect us if we have turned our backs on God. Children are not stupid. They see how we live our private lives. They are turned off by hypocrisy.

If we allow God to live His life in us, we are faithful to what He tells us to do, we look always to His Word for guidance and we attempt to lead our children in the ways of the Lord, He will be with us and help us. Just watch and see what wonders God will do in your family when you live in this way.

Children are a blank slate that we can draw on. We must lead them into the right paths:

> *Train up a child in the way he should go: and when he is old, he will not depart from it.*
>   Proverbs 22:6

Studies have repeatedly shown that the first seven years of a child's life are crucial to his future development. These are the years in which children develop many of their belief patterns, and this is the critical period for religious training. Children need to be taught, and they need to experience what it means to live life in Christ. They need to learn values, and to see their parents living their lives as examples of those values.

Children need to learn that there is a God who created them. They need to understand that God loves them and has a plan for their lives. They must come to know the Gospel and what Jesus Christ has done on their behalf. They should be able to tell others about Jesus and about why they believe in Him. They should learn by example the value of a life that is given to serving the Lord and other people.

It is my strong belief that children should be carefully taught, and God has given the task to parents, not to Sunday schools, Christian schools or religious clubs. This is our job, and we must be mature enough to do it:

> *Wherewithal shall a young man cleanse his way? by taking heed thereto according to thy word. With my whole heart have I sought thee: O let me not wander from thy commandments. Thy word have I hid in mine heart, that I might not sin against thee. Blessed art thou, O LORD: teach me thy statutes. With my lips have I declared all the judgments of thy mouth. I have rejoiced in the way of thy testimonies, as much as in all riches. I will meditate in thy precepts, and have respect unto thy ways. I will delight myself in thy statutes: I will not forget thy word.* Psalm 119:9-16

It is only as we parents cleanse our own ways, heeding the Word of God and serving Him wholeheartedly, allowing nothing to cause us to wander from His commandments, that we can successfully train up our children in the way they should go. It is not enough to teach them Bible stories and Bible doctrines. We must instill the fear of the Lord and the knowledge of the Word within their hearts and spirits:

> *And all thy children shall be taught of the LORD;*
> *and great shall be the peace of thy children.*
>   Isaiah 54:13

God is calling His Church to raise up godly families made up of individuals that love and respect each other. He is calling for families who will stand as examples in the community and will draw in many others who have no family influence or poor family influence. Because of this, He is calling us to bring our family life into order, so that we can help those whose families are in chaos. He is calling us to be those who walk in the Word, displaying His life to the world.

Walking in God's ways will bring healing to families, and as family after family is healed, this will produce *Healing for the Nations.*

THE POWER OF PREACHING THE GOSPEL

And he said unto them, Go ye into all the world, and preach the gospel to every creature.

Mark 16:15

And Jesus came and spake unto them, saying, All power is given unto me in heaven and in earth. Go ye therefore, and teach all nations, baptizing them in the name of the Father, and of the Son, and of the Holy Ghost: Teaching them to observe all things whatsoever I have commanded you: and, lo, I am with you alway, even unto the end of the world. Amen. Matthew 28:18-20

We are all familiar with the passage

known as the Great Commission. It contains Jesus' last words to His disciples before He left this Earth. Nothing could be more important, for nothing can replace the power of the Gospel to change men's lives. God has given us His Word, and that Word contains the answers to the world's problems. The Lord Jesus Christ has commissioned us to go into all the world and preach this good news *"to every creature."* The triumphant and living Lord has sent His ambassadors forth to proclaim His Word throughout all the world.

The Great Commission, therefore, is not a choice. It is a command for every believer. All power and authority in Heaven and on Earth are now in the hands of our Lord Jesus Christ and on the basis of that authority and power Christians, Christ's representatives, have been commissioned to carry out His work. The Great Commission is not something to be carried out only by those called as missionaries to other countries. It is something to which every believer is called. Wherever we go, we are to teach and preach the good news of Christ.

What is it that the Great Commission requires of us? We are to *"go"* and we are to *"preach the Gospel."* We are to go where people are in need of help, and we are to give them God's message.

The Gospel has the power to change men's lives. Paul wrote:

The Power of Preaching the Gospel

For I am not ashamed of the gospel of Christ: for it is the power of God unto salvation to every one that believeth; to the Jew first, and also to the Greek.   Romans 1:16

What is the Gospel? It is the good news that Christ died so that we might live. It is His Word, His story, His proclamation to the world.

Peter was preaching the Gospel when he said:

Repent, and be baptized every one of you in the name of Jesus Christ for the remission of sins.
                                             Acts 2:38

This is the good news that men and women can receive *"the remission of sins."* This blessing comes as a person believes the Gospel, repents of his sins and is baptized. The Gospel brought about a total change in the lives of those who heard Peter preach that day, and they became spiritual creatures:

And they continued stedfastly in the apostles' doctrine and fellowship, and in breaking of bread, and in prayers.   Acts 2:42

This same total change came to people everywhere the disciples preached and because the Gospel has this power to change men's lives, we have a serious job to do. We must spread this news far and wide.

The Gospel is the story of Nicodemus and the truths Jesus taught about the born-again experience:

> *There was a man of the Pharisees, named Nicodemus, a ruler of the Jews: The same came to Jesus by night, and said unto him, Rabbi, we know that thou art a teacher come from God: for no man can do these miracles that thou doest, except God be with him.*
>
> *Jesus answered and said unto him, Verily, verily, I say unto thee, Except a man be born again, he cannot see the kingdom of God.*
>
> *Nicodemus saith unto him, How can a man be born when he is old? can he enter the second time into his mother's womb, and be born?*
>
> *Jesus answered, Verily, verily, I say unto thee, Except a man be born of water and of the Spirit, he cannot enter into the kingdom of God. That which is born of the flesh is flesh; and that which is born of the Spirit is spirit. Marvel not that I said unto thee, Ye must be born again. The wind bloweth where it listeth, and thou hearest the sound thereof, but canst not tell whence it cometh, and whither it goeth: so is every one that is born of the Spirit.*   John 3:1-8

Each of us must take time to learn some of the powerful promises in God's Word that lead men and women to salvation. Then we can encourage others in their time of need. For example, here are a few good ones to learn:

Look unto me, and be ye saved, all the ends of the earth: for I am God, and there is none else.

Isaiah 45:22

If thou shalt confess with thy mouth the Lord Jesus, and shalt believe in thine heart that God hath raised him from the dead, thou shalt be saved. For with the heart man believeth unto righteousness; and with the mouth confession is made unto salvation. For the scripture saith, Whosoever believeth on him shall not be ashamed.

Romans 10:9-11

But without faith it is impossible to please him: for he that cometh to God must believe that he is, and that he is a rewarder of them that diligently seek him.

Hebrews 11:6

If we say that we have no sin, we deceive ourselves, and the truth is not in us. If we confess our sins, he is faithful and just to forgive us our sins, and to cleanse us from all unrighteousness.

1 John 1:8-9

For as the heaven is high above the earth, so great is his mercy toward them that fear him. As far as

the east is from the west, so far hath he removed
our transgressions from us. Like as a father pitieth
his children, so the LORD *pitieth them that fear*
him.   Psalm 103:11-13

The Gospel is much more than salvation. As the disciples of the first century preached the Gospel, other things happened. Sick people were healed. Those who were demon possessed were delivered. Dead people were even raised to life again. These same signs should follow the preaching of the Gospel today. We are still to bring God's healing to the sick and suffering. We are still to cast out demons. God has given us this authority as part of our commission.

Our ministry today is an extension of the ministry of Jesus on the Earth. When He stood one day in the synagogue of Nazareth, He read to the people from the prophecy of Isaiah and said that He and His ministry were the fulfillment of it:

And there was delivered unto him the book of the
prophet Esaias. And when he had opened the book,
he found the place where it was written, The Spirit
of the Lord is upon me, because he hath anointed
me to preach the gospel to the poor; he hath sent
me to heal the brokenhearted, to preach deliver-
ance to the captives, and recovering of sight to
the blind, to set at liberty them that are bruised,

The Power of Preaching the Gospel

and we can be a part of His triumph as we are faithful in the our personal witness and in the preaching of the Gospel. We can be a part of God's plan of *Healing for the Nations.*

PART III:

THE METHOD FOR HEALING

Part III:

The Method for Healing

AMERICA THE BACKSLIDER, ARISE TO LEAD THE NATIONS TO HEALING

Go and proclaim these words toward the north, and say, Return, thou backsliding Israel, saith the LORD; and I will not cause mine anger to fall upon you: for I am merciful, saith the LORD, and I will not keep anger for ever.   Jeremiah 3:12

*F*or many decades now, the United States of America has been a beacon of freedom for the rest of the world. While chaos has reigned in many parts of the Earth, we have enjoyed relative peace and unparalleled prosperity here in this land. We therefore have a responsibility to the rest of the world. We must show them the way.

Many have attributed our blessing to our freedoms, which are considerable. Our greatest freedom, however, is the ability to practice our faith in the way we choose. It is faith in God, not any other factor, that has made America great.

It has been because of our faith in God and our knowledge of His teachings that America has historically been able to take a leading role in presenting an example of godly, honest and moral living before the world and of spreading the Gospel of the Lord Jesus Christ to the ends of the Earth.

God's blessings have been upon America because America was a praying country. We must not lose that distinction. This is the reason it has been so alarming to many that prayer has been taken out of our public schools. Should we wonder that there is so much crime in the classroom? Children are taking guns and knives and drugs into the schools, and officials respond by setting up metal detectors and conducting random searches of students to help prevent violence. Children are shooting and killing one another, even in our schools. Too late, many are beginning to realize what a mistake it was to permit the removal of the powerful weapon of prayer from our classrooms.

Those who control our American schools have been deceived. While they were looking at students' "rights" and turning a deaf ear to the cries for righteousness that arose, sin swept into our schools to engulf our children like a flood. Now, to try to decrease teenage pregnancy, authorities have begun distributing condoms in schools. This has only led to a further increase in sexual activity by teenagers. While no one can be against using condoms as a means of protecting oneself against the spread of venereal diseases, does it make any sense to remove the very best protection we could have — prayer — and replace it with condoms?

Obedience to God is the very best protection against promiscuity, the spread of sexually-transmitted diseases and the rise of teenage birthrates. Obedience to God is the best protection against drug use and against the threat of violence in our schools.

Many of the things we are suffering in our society at large are the result of our backsliding as a nation, of our having left our first love, Jesus Christ. As we have seen, *"the way of transgressors is hard"* (Proverbs 13:15).

The Old Testament history of Israel can teach us much in this regard, for Israel too was a backsliding nation:

> *Hast thou seen that which backsliding Israel hath done? she is gone up upon every high mountain and under every green tree, and there hath played the harlot.*   Jeremiah 3:6

God did not forsake Israel or turn from her. He

pleaded with her, through the prophet Jeremiah, to return to Him:

> *Go and proclaim these words toward the north, and say, Return, thou backsliding Israel, saith the LORD; and I will not cause mine anger to fall upon you: for I am merciful, saith the LORD, and I will not keep anger for ever. Only acknowledge thine iniquity, that thou has transgressed against the LORD thy God, and hast scattered thy ways to the strangers under every green tree, and ye have not obeyed my voice, saith the LORD. Turn, O backsliding children, saith the LORD; for I am married unto you: and I will take you one of a city, and two of a family, and I will bring you to Zion: And I will give you pastors according to mine heart, which shall feed you with knowledge and understanding.* Jeremiah 3:12-15

When we consider the goodness of God toward America, the fact that most of us have food on our tables, clothes to wear, and shoes on our feet should cause us to recognize our need of God and to turn back to Him. Just as we enjoy many freedoms in the natural, we can also be free spiritually. We do not need to live under bondage to demonic spirits. As a backsliding nation, we can turn back to God.

The word "backslide" simply means "turning back" or "turning away." Backsliding means that we have become stubborn and rebellious and refuse to do things God's way. Just as the Israelites were prone to backsliding as they marched out of the slavery of Egypt and pressed toward their unseen Promised Land, so are we all tempted to backslide, to turn to the world instead of to God, to return to Egypt and what we are accustomed to.

God has not forsaken the backslider. In the moment that we are willing again to repent of our wrongdoing, to listen to His voice, and to follow Him anew, He is there waiting for us with outstretched arms. Despite the fact that the people of Israel rebelled time and time again, God still loved them, still called them, and still forgave them when they willingly turned to Him. As believers in Christ, we have been grafted into the true vine. God has given us a wonderful opportunity to partake of His blessings. The fact that we have not appreciated His blessings and have gone our own way has not lessened His love. He is reaching out to us today, ready to heal our nation. He has said:

> *If my people, which are called by my name, shall humble themselves, and pray, and seek my face, and turn from their wicked ways; then will I hear from heaven, and will forgive their sin, and will heal their land.* 2 Chronicles 7:14

Isaiah warned the children of Israel that God

would not always be available to them and that they should seek Him *"while He may be found"*:

> *Seek ye the* LORD *while he may be found, call ye upon him while he is near: Let the wicked forsake his way, and the unrighteous man his thoughts: and let him return unto the* LORD, *and he will have mercy upon him; and to our God, for he will abundantly pardon.*　　　　Isaiah 55:6-7

In the same breath in which he declared that we must seek God *"while He may be found,"* Isaiah gave us a recipe of sorts for returning from backsliding:

> *Let the wicked forsake his* [own wilful] *way.*
> *Let ... the unrighteous man* [forsake] *his* [own wilful] *thoughts.*
> *Let him return unto the Lord.*

When we are willing to do our part, Isaiah showed us, God will indeed respond to us:

> *He will have mercy upon him ...*
> *He will abundantly pardon.*

God is calling America to repentance. He is saying, as He did to backsliding Israel:

> *Ho, every one that thirsteth, come ye to the waters, and he that hath no money; come ye, buy*

and eat; yea, come, buy wine and milk without money and without price. Wherefore do ye spend money for that which is not bread? and your labour for that which satisfieth not? hearken diligently unto me, and eat ye that which is good, and let your soul delight itself in fatness. Incline your ear, and come unto me: hear, and your soul shall live; and I will make an everlasting covenant with you, even the sure mercies of David.

Isaiah 55:1-3

One of the difficulties we face in modern American society is our high level of education. We have become so proud, so self-reliant, so sure of ourselves. God said through Isaiah:

For my thoughts are not your thoughts, neither are your ways my ways, saith the LORD. For as the heavens are higher than the earth, so are my ways higher than your ways, and my thoughts than your thoughts.   Isaiah 55:8-9

Because of our pride and arrogance, we are in danger of losing the blessings of God. How could we have taken God out of our schools and put the devil in His place? America was founded upon the principles of the Word of God. How could we have replaced them? Suddenly, black has become white and white has become black; right has become wrong and wrong has become right. Lies have become more popular than the truth. This is dangerous. Somehow our minds have become corrupted. The Apostle Paul described us well when he said:

> *Because that, when they knew God, they glorified him not as God, neither were thankful; but became vain in their imaginations, and their foolish heart was darkened. Professing themselves to be wise, they became fools, And changed the glory of the incorruptible God into an image made like to corruptible man, and to birds, and fourfooted beasts, and creeping things.* Romans 1:21-23

This is a very dangerous position to be in, as Paul went on to show:

> *Wherefore God also gave them up to uncleanness through the lusts of their own hearts, to dishonour their own bodies between themselves: Who changed the truth of God into a lie, and worshipped and served the creature more than the Creator, who is blessed for ever. Amen.*
> Romans 1:24-25

This explains some of the things we read each day in our newspapers and hear on the television news:

> *For this cause God gave them up unto vile affections: for even their women did change the natural*

*use into that which is against nature: And like-
wise also the men, leaving the natural use of the
woman, burned in their lust one toward another;
men with men working that which is unseemly,
and receiving in themselves that recompence of
their error which was meet.*   Romans 1:26-27

There is no way we can blame God for all this
mess. It is due to our own backsliding:

*And even as they did not like to retain God in the
knowledge, God gave them over to a reprobate
mind, to do those things which are not convenient;
Being filled with all unrighteousness, fornication,
wickedness, covetousness, maliciousness; full of
envy, murder, debate, deceit, malignity; whisper-
ers, backbiters, haters of God, despiteful, proud,
boasters, inventors of evil things, disobedient to
parents. Without understanding, covenant-break-
ers, without natural affection, implacable,
unmerciful.*   Romans 1:28-31

This is not a legacy to be proud of. God declared
judgment on those who insisted on their rebellious
ways. This chapter ends with a warning:

*Who knowing the judgment of God, that they
which commit such things are worthy of death,*

not only do the same, but have pleasure in them that do them. Romans 1:32

America, it is time for repentance, time to recognize our backsliding as a nation and to turn wholly back to our God. If we will only turn to the Lord, He will forgive us of our sins, and surely He will have mercy and pardon:

> *A voice was heard upon the high places, weeping and supplications of the children of Israel: for they have perverted their way, and they have forgotten the LORD their God. Return, ye backsliding children, and I will heal your backslidings. Behold, we come unto thee; for thou art the LORD our God.* Jeremiah 3:21-22

It is time to return to the Lord. We can then lead the way in bringing *Healing for the Nations.*

GETTING GOD'S GLORY INTO YOUR OWN LIFE

*The hand of the LORD was upon me, and carried
me out in the spirit of the LORD, and set me down
in the midst of the valley which was full of bones,
And caused me to pass by them round about: and,
behold, there were very many in the open valley;
and, lo, they were very dry. And he said unto me,
Son of man, can these bones live? And I answered,
O Lord GOD, thou knowest.* Ezekiel 37:1-3

efore we can bless the people
around us, we must have God's glory in our own
souls. Ezekiel was a man deeply burdened with his
responsibility for the nation of Israel, but before he

could be a blessing to the nation, he had to have *"the hand of the Lord"* upon his own life.

Even Jesus had to maintain His spiritual life while He was on the Earth. He brought life and healing wherever He went because He consistently sought the Father and did His will. He said that He did nothing that He did not see His Father doing in Heaven:

> *Then answered Jesus and said unto them, Verily, verily, I say unto you, The Son can do nothing of himself, but what he seeth the Father do: for what things soever he doeth, these also doeth the Son likewise. For the Father loveth the Son, and showeth him all things that himself doeth: and he will show him greater works than these, that ye may marvel.* John 5:19-20

Jesus not only lived a life of prayer, but he also lived a life of seeing into the heavenlies and of hearing from His Father. He is our example.

God hasn't changed. He speaks to His people just as He did to the prophets of old and to the first-century believers. If we learn to quiet ourselves before Him, He will speak to us and show us things we did not know. He gives us His direction, confirming it by His Word.

Our God longs to reveal His heart to His people. He will show those who seek Him the great and deep things hidden in His heart. His secrets are for those who walk in intimate companionship with Him. He has promised:

> *Surely the Lord GOD will do nothing, but he revealeth his secret unto his servants the prophets. The lion hath roared, who will not fear? the Lord GOD hath spoken, who can but prophesy?*
> Amos 3:7-8

> *The secret of the LORD is with them that fear him; and he will show them his covenant.*
> Psalm 25:14

The prophets of old were great because of their intimate walk with the Lord. The apostles of the first century were powerful because they had been with Jesus.

Ezekiel became a great prophet of God, but it was only because of *"the hand of the Lord"* on his life. Ezekiel believed for bones to be raised to life again, but only because *"the hand of the Lord"* was upon his life. Ezekiel prophesied to those bones and saw them supernaturally raised up, but only because of *"the hand of the Lord"* that was upon his life.

We can only bless other people in the proportion that we have been blessed. We can only give what we have received. It is only as we get into the glory ourselves that we can be able to take that glory out to the nations.

God's glory comes upon us as we allow the Holy Ghost power to work in our hearts and lives. Jesus promised:

> *But ye shall receive power, after that the Holy Ghost is come upon you: and ye shall be witnesses unto me both in Jerusalem, and in all Judaea, and in Samaria, and unto the uttermost part of the earth.* Acts 1:8

> *But when the Comforter is come, whom I will send unto you from the Father, even the Spirit of truth, which proceedeth from the Father, he shall testify of me: And ye also shall bear witness, because ye have been with me from the beginning.* John 15:26-27

God's power in us does two wonderful things. It makes us able to be overcomers ourselves, and it gives us power to bless those around us. It is the power of the Holy Ghost that will enable us to bless the world.

Stop worrying about how dry the bones in the churchyard seem to be. Get God's glory in your own soul, and you will be able to raise dead bones to life. Stop worrying about how backslidden and spiritually impoverished the world seems to be. Get God's glory in your soul, and you can help to change all that.

Getting God's Glory Into Your Own Life

God is breathing new life into His Church. He is raising up dead things. He is forming a mighty army of His chosen ones. Will you take your place in the ranks of His servants? Let revival come to your own soul today, and you will be used of God to bring forth *Healing for the Nations.*

BRINGING GOD'S GLORY TO THE NATIONS

And he showed me a pure river of water of life, clear as crystal, proceeding out of the throne of God and of the Lamb. In the midst of the street of it, and on either side of the river, was there the tree of life, which bare twelve manner of fruits, and yielded her fruit every month: and the leaves of the tree were FOR THE HEALING OF THE NATIONS.　Revelation 22:1-2

*G*od is ready to bless America and every other nation that will seek Him. He has already prepared the leaves *"for the healing of the nations."* That healing process is just waiting for us to act.

Healing for the Nations is not a difficult thing for God. Negative circumstances don't hinder Him. Wars and rumors of wars don't hinder Him. Nothing can hinder God. His plan will be carried out, and nothing will prevent His will from being accomplished. But will we have a part in it? We can — if we are willing.

If we are willing to accept the responsibility of intercessory prayer and to pay the price in time and effort to take our loved ones and friends and neighbors before the throne of God, we can bring forth *Healing for the Nations.*

If we are willing to declare war on Satan and his kingdom, to stand against his desires and to reveal his tricks, we can bring forth *Healing for the Nations.*

If we are willing to lay aside our petty differences and join hands with one another in the family of God, we can bring forth *Healing for the Nations.*

If we are willing to first be partakers of the message by dedicating ourselves to righteous living, we can bring forth *Healing for the Nations.*

If we are willing to accept the challenge to go to those who are hurting and dying and carry to them the good news of Jesus' love, we can bring forth *Healing for the Nations.*

Are you ready to be a witness? Are you ready to let your own life be an example to others? Are you ready to give yourself to the Word? Are you ready to fast and pray? If so, you are a candidate for God's service.

Get ready to bless others. Get ready to lay your hands on sick people and see them healed. Get ready to see many lost souls come to Christ. Get ready to cast out devils. Get ready to speak the word of faith. Get ready to see walls crumble and cities taken. This is God's time. Get ready.

Do you still doubt that God can heal the nations? John saw something wonderful when he was in the Spirit on the Lord's day:

> *After this I beheld, and, lo, a great multitude, which no man could number, of all nations, and kindreds, and people, and tongues, stood before the throne, and before the Lamb, clothed with white robes, and palms in their hands; And cried with a loud voice, saying, Salvation to our God which sitteth upon the throne, and unto the Lamb.*
>
> Revelation 7:9-10

Who did he say was there? *"A GREAT MULTITUDE."*

Where were those people from? *"OF ALL NATIONS AND KINDREDS AND PEOPLE AND TONGUES."*

What was their appearance? They were *"CLOTHED WITH WHITE ROBES."*

What were they saying? *"SALVATION TO OUR GOD."*

What more do we need? It will indeed happen and we are on the threshold of it. God is ready to pour out of His Spirit upon all flesh.

Don't let anything hinder you in this important hour. Jesus prophesied of the attitude of many:

> *And then shall many be offended, and shall betray one another, and shall hate one another.*
> Matthew 24:10

These are the last days of which Jesus spoke. All around us, we see the signs. This, however, is not a time for wavering. Stand firm in the faith. Don't dare be among those who are falling away.

Stop expecting bad things to happen in your life. Bad things will happen to the world, but God's people should expect great things. Expect the power of God to come upon you in new ways. Expect to speak in tongues and prophesy and see signs and wonders and miracles in your life everyday. Expect to bask in the presence of the Lord. Expect to receive revelation from Heaven. Expect to hear the voice of God.

Expect to experience the river of God. Expect to see the trees that line its banks. Expect to benefit from the *"twelve manner of fruits"* and from the leaves that are *"FOR THE HEALING OF THE NATIONS."* If you will believe for it, God will do it for you.

The course of nations rests within your hands. God has called you to expand His Kingdom by sharing His glory with the people around you, at home and abroad. You have it within your power to affect the entire world for good.

When God spoke to Jeremiah concerning the destiny of nations, He said:

> *O house of Israel, cannot I do with you as this potter? saith the* LORD. *Behold, as the clay is in the potter's hand, so are ye in mine hand, O house of Israel. At what instant I shall speak concerning a nation, and concerning a kingdom, to pluck up, and to pull down, and to destroy it; If that nation, against whom I have pronounced, turn from their evil, I will repent of the evil that I thought to do unto them. And at what instant I shall speak concerning a nation, and concerning a kingdom, to build and to plant it; If it do evil in my sight, that it obey not my voice, then I will repent of the good, wherewith I said I would benefit them. Now therefore go to, speak to the men of Judah, and to the inhabitants of Jerusalem, saying, Thus saith the* LORD; *Behold, I frame evil against you, and devise a device against you: return ye now every one from his evil way, and make your ways and your doings good.*
>
> Jeremiah 18:6-11

God has not changed, and nations still rise and fall in relationship to their response to Him. Just as

He spoke to His prophet Jeremiah so long ago, God is speaking to you today and calling you forth as a prophetic voice to speak to the people and to the nations, that the destiny of individuals and families and communities might be decided. Will you hear Him today? Will you bring forth *Healing for the Nations*?

And he showed me a pure river of water of life, clear as crystal, proceeding out of the throne of God and of the Lamb. In the midst of the street of it, and on either side of the river, was there the tree of life, which bare twelve manner of fruits, and yielded her fruit every month: and the leaves of the tree were FOR THE HEALING OF THE NATIONS. Revelation 22:1-2

ABOUT THE AUTHOR

Dr. Gertrude Dixon is a native of Miami, Florida, where she received her early education in the public schools. Later, she met and married Joseph B. T. Dixon, Jr. of Hagerstown, Maryland. A year and a half after their marriage, she accepted the Lord Jesus Christ as her personal Savior and was immediately called by God into the ministry. She studied, beginning in 1968, at Washington Bible Extension School, through Heritage Academy in Hagerstown.

In 1983 she enrolled in Hagerstown Community College to pursue a degree in Social Work, then did two years of studies at Antietam Bible College and graduated.

Dr. Dixon earned her Bachelor of Theology degree from Calvary Bible College and Seminary in Pasasdena, Texas. She earned her Master of Arts degree in Christian Counseling Psychology and her Doctor of Philosophy in Christian Counseling Psychology from Cornerstone University in Lake Charles, Louisiana. She is a licensed Clinical Christian Counselor and is a member of the National Christian Counselors' Association based in Sarasota, Florida.

Dr. Dixon is founder and pastor of The Capital Heights Revival Center Holiness Church of God in Martinsburg, West Virginia, where she has served for twenty-one years. She has been an instrument of God used to feed the hungry in Martinsburg, Hagerstown and other surrounding areas. God has also used her to preach deliverance to the captives in many cities of our country and in several foreign countries as well. Many souls have been saved, healed and freed from oppression in her ministry. She is currently being called to speak in ministers' conferences in many parts of the United States. She gives all the glory to God.

Dr. Dixon was blessed by God to go to the Holy Land in 1996 and was called upon to preach aboard a boat on the Sea of Galilee, where Jesus did many of His miracles. She was baptized in the River Jordan and walked in many of the other places where Jesus walked. She also visited the sites of the seven churches of Asia.

Dr. Dixon's first book, *Counseled by the Spirit,* was published in 1996. The book dealt with the subject of Christian counseling and was subtitled *Bringing Healing to the Lives of Hurting People.* She is grateful to God for His goodness to her and for giving her the joy of helping hurting people from all walks of life through her ministry. She is believing for God's *Healing for the Nations.*

You may contact the author by writing:

Dr. Gertrude Dixon
1105 Kuhn Avenue
Hagerstown, MD 21742